Stephen Cherry is Director of Ministerial Development and Parish Support in the diocese of Durham, and a Residentiary Canon of Durham Cathedral. His publications include *Barefoot Disciple: Walking the Way of Passionate Humility* (the Archbishop of Canterbury's Lent Book, 2011), *Healing Agony: Reimagining Forgiveness* and *Beyond Busyness: Time Wisdom for Ministry*.

Like the sound of working through this book with others around the world?

Want to be inspired in your discipleship journey through poetry, creativity and input from a range of voices over Lent?

Want to delve into the Bible with your cell group, and share some of those conversations with others through social media?

JOIN THE BIG READ FOR LENT 2014!

Think about how deeply you'd like to be involved and choose from the following options:

- just read the book;
- download FREE house-group study materials from **http://bigbible. org.uk/big-read/bigread14**, a menu which includes Nibbles (conversation starters); Main Course (Bible materials, author videos, reflections, questions); Dessert (a prayerful activity); After Dinner Chocs (something to take away and sink your teeth into, or suck on, over the week);
- participate in a Facebook group (**http://j.mp/FBBigRead**) sharing ideas and discussing Big Read themes, or through Twitter using the hashtag **#bigread14**;
- take advantage of tips, tricks, interviews and training in social media (materials can be found via **http://bigbible.org.uk/digilit/**) in order to contribute online through word, image or sound;
- Participate in **#Do1NiceThing** each day, in activities inspired by the poems, provided by Love Your Streets (Street Angels).

Materials related to The Big Read 2014, and opportunities to engage with it, can be accessed via **http://bigbible.org.uk/tag/bigread14/**. *The daily readings start on 2 March 2014, with Ash Wednesday (the official start of Lent) on 5 March. Lent finishes on 17 April 2014, with the readings finishing on 26 April.*

BAREFOOT PRAYERS

A meditation a day for
Lent and Easter

Stephen Cherry

First published in Great Britain in 2013

Society for Promoting Christian Knowledge
36 Causton Street
London SW1P 4ST
www.spckpublishing.co.uk

British Library Cataloguing-in-Publication Data
A catalogue record for this book is available from the British Library

ISBN 978–0–281–07125–8
eBook ISBN 978–0–281–07126–5

eBook by Graphicraft Limited, Hong Kong

Typeset by Graphicraft Limited, Hong Kong
Manufacture managed by Jellyfish
First printed in Great Britain by CPI Group
Subsequently digitally printed in Great Britain

Produced on paper from sustainable forests

For Rachel: daughter, friend and companion

The voice of prayer is never silent.
John Ellerton

Contents

━━━━━━━━◆◆◆━━━━━━━━

Contents

Week 3
Occasions

Week 4
Puzzles

Week 5
Responses

Contents

Week 6
Virtues

Week 7
Deeps

Week 8
Horizons

An introduction in three parts

The voice of prayer

Prayer is an extremely common human activity. As John Ellerton put it in a famous hymn, 'the voice of prayer is never silent / nor dies the strain of praise away'.[1] It takes myriad forms and transpires in countless contexts. Yet it is also strange and riddled with paradox. We associate it with our deepest peace, but it is often anguished – and edgy.

Prayer happens at the boundaries of meaning, and often comes from us when we are at our wits' end. We pray when we would like to take control of events but know we cannot. We pray when we would like to get a grip on something quite uncontrollable. We pray when we are perplexed and when there is no convincing plan. These are not the only times we pray. But it is at such times that we are likely to pray in the spirit of handing over to God what in truth we care about deeply.

Personal prayer often has something of an anarchic quality about it. It lives beyond the scope of the doctrinal, metaphysical or rational police. It is informed by the less tameable parts of our person – our will, our desire, our fear, our imagination and both our worthy and our less worthy longings. Prayer can also spring from the compassion and anger that happen when we see the suffering of others. Empathy is the driver of intercessory prayer – empathy in the company of hope. These are beautiful parts of human nature, but they are not safe. Rather they are lively and, where there is injustice, discontent. Protest is an important part of the honesty of prayer – and we should expect to hear its discordant notes from time to time.

* * *

The word 'spirituality' is a highly attractive one: infinitely more attractive than 'religion' and more liberating than 'prayer'. To pin it down by definition is perhaps to miss the point of the word, to forget why the word itself is so compelling today. It is about the undefinable, the untameable, and the unorganiz-able. Inasmuch as God is all these things, spirituality can be about God. More importantly, anything that is, as it were, about God must be touched by something of these qualities. There is no God without spirituality in some sense, for, as Jesus says in John's Gospel, 'God is spirit' (John 4.24).

One traditional and wise way of seeking to avoid the error of suggesting that we can control things of the Spirit is to think and talk *negatively*. Such an approach makes me want to suggest that spirituality is the task of *not* inhibiting the grace – or Spirit – of God. Much prayer is a huge exercise in getting over yourself. In a famous sermon Paul Tillich urged his con-gregations to 'simply accept the fact that you are accepted'.[2] If acceptance would only come about as a result of ministerial instruction, then life would be a lot more straightforward than it is. Walter Brueggemann was nearer the mark when he realized that human beings are not changed by ethical urging but by transformed imagination.[3] Prayer is in part the project of letting our imagination be transformed by God's Spirit acting in us and through us. As such it involves a special kind of effort: the effort of not making an effort.

The paradox involved here is well expressed by Robert Llewellyn, who talks about the value, when dealing with distrac-tions in prayer, of two sentences: 'Do not try to think' and 'Do not try not to think'.[4] It is the space, the poise, between these two sentences that I am trying to describe: the effort of spirituality is the effort of getting yourself out of the way.

This is the opposite of what we might first think when we embark along a spiritual path.

Typically, people today see spirituality as a way towards personal fulfilment. As they do so, one of the images that might be in their minds is that of Albert Maslow's well-known 'Hierarchy of Needs'.[5] Maslow suggests that human beings have several layers of need, the lowest of which is biological – food, water, shelter – rising through layers such as 'safety', 'belonging' and 'esteem' to 'self-actualization', at the top of a pyramid.

Authentic Christian spirituality does not see it like that. It sees spirituality as something that pervades the whole of life and is there within the material level of need as well as at every other level. In fact, Christianity's disagreement with Maslow is most intense at the very top of the pyramid. To frame life as the pursuit of 'self-actualization' is far too individualistic and, to be blunt, selfish to square with Christian values in general and the gospel of Jesus Christ in particular. At the top of the Christian pyramid is not self-actualization but *self-giving*. What exactly that is and why it is *more than fulfilling* is something that is hard to explain – something we only realize through spiritual intuition and faithful and generous living. Living out of that intuition is what we call faith. It is not the pursuit of self-fulfilment as if that were intrinsically good, or of 'peak experiences' as if their value was self-evident and self-contained.

* * *

When St Paul wrote of praying with sighs too deep for words (Romans 8.26) he revealed something constant about the human spirit: we do not have the words to contain our prayers. We never have and we never will. True prayer breaks the bounds of language. It always has and it always will. There can be prayer

3

in instrumental music and I know people who deliberately and wordlessly dance their prayers. Maybe this is why some of the most common prayer-words, like 'Alleluia' and 'Amen', are happily used by people who have little or no sense of their literal meaning.

Prayer is not something we do. It is what God does in and through us. It is the Spirit in our hearts. It is the Spirit's inarticulate groans and sighs, which are often too deep for words yet somehow, sometimes, verbal.

We pray in the same way as a clarinet sounds: as the breath of another passes through us. We pray in the same way that a harp sings: when someone plucks our strings. We pray, sometimes, as the drum declaims when struck by hand or stick and we make a bang or a boom. To pray is to make a sound, more than, or before, it is to make a thought. The voice of prayer is never silent: but it is often without words.

Poets speak of the muse that may or may not be there for them. This is an apt metaphor for the Spirit. It cannot be conjured up. It blows where it will (John 3.8). There is no possibility of controlling it; the best we can do is cooperate and collaborate. And that is absolutely the best we can do. To be in tune with God's Spirit, to let God's Spirit call the tune from the instrument that we are: this is the height of Christian spirituality, Christian living, and Christian service.

Prayer requires a strange blend of dispositions: self-forgetful presence and absorption. It is self-aware but not self-conscious. As soon as the self becomes interested in itself, or drawn towards prideful self-regard or abject self-loathing, the moment of prayer has passed. Only the self-accepting person can pray, and yet it is the person who cannot accept him or herself who most needs to pray.

Although prayer itself is not self-conscious, people who pray will often experience several layers of self-consciousness. This is normal and natural and not to be worried about, though it is also, to be frank, a bit of a nuisance. God is very close to us and yet not manifest in any obvious way. So when we go looking for God it is very likely that we will find not God but ourselves, or some aspect of ourselves. It may be our recent memories, it might be a digestive problem or headache or the realization that we cannot get comfortable. As we get beyond that we encounter our worries – what we have yet to do today, what we did not do so well yesterday. Beyond them, we encounter our desires and the dream world of our fantasies. All bets are off as to what might happen now. And yet true prayer is neither about settling at any of these levels nor battling with them, but rather letting them all fall away: forgetting them as we pay calm attention not to the trumpet-call of our now rather irritated self, but to the breathy sound of the Spirit that has always been praying through us but which we have drowned out by the cacophony of self-regard that is our normal waking state.

It follows that prayer requires of us real patience. 'Be patient and without resentment,' wrote Rilke to a young poet in the days leading up to Christmas.[6] The same advice might be passed to someone who wants to pray or to develop in Christian spirituality. Resentment can get in the way of prayer, especially if it's self-regarding and petty – which it often is. But patience is the main thing. Some things can't be hurried. We need to wait for them to happen. They cannot be forced. Prayer is not a strain, but a response to grace. It is not us rolling up our sleeves to get on with it, but us waiting patiently and expectantly and inviting God to do God's thing in God's time. We can only pray when we let go of the desire, deep-seated in us though it is, to control; when we remember that we are not God.

* * *

Poetry is the natural idiom of any prayer that has become verbal. Prose prayers are possible, so too are list-prayers. But it is the poem-prayer that is the most natural and comfortable form – which is why Psalms and hymns and spiritual songs are so central in the Christian tradition (Ephesians 5.19). What the Psalms achieve over and above the hymns and songs is to remain in touch with the wildness of the grace of God and the actual pain of the human soul. They do so in ways that are not tidied up to fit in with the disciplines of metre or rhyme or to sound nice when sung in worship.

A good poem, it is said, is felt, is experienced, before it is understood. In this way a poem is like a person. We can enter into a relationship with it, finding it unfathomable and inexhaustible and irreducible. A poem is not a code. It is the shape and sound as well as the meaning of the words of which it is made. Poetry is language understood sacramentally: it conveys not just meaning but grace, and therefore speaks of plenitude and peace.

A poem that is also a prayer has inevitably been invested with a certain amount of subjectivity by the one who made it. The fact that the making of it was not experienced as a deliberate, controlled or planned act of creation, as the exercise of power or authority, is neither here nor there. The poem that lives was living even as it was conceived.

This is also true of our everyday, unwritten and unreflected prayer. It is out there, prayed, done, before we have got the meaning, the thought, even the intention, straight in our minds. It's not that we have a lofty thought and then struggle to find the right words. Or if it is like that, then it's the exception. More likely the word – or even the sound – comes first. Like when we drop something heavy on our foot and hear ourselves spitting out an exclamation we are not proud of. So it is with prayer from the heart, prayer in the Spirit. It has to be, for it is only in this way that we give voice to rough protestation, raw praise and unfettered lamentation. True prayer is necessarily unguarded and unrefined. It *is* rough and raw, and reveals to us something about what is going on at the deeper level where God connects with us.

If this sounds very different from the effort of writing a sonnet or even a limerick, it is. To pray is an art and to make prayers is a craft. But it is the most artless of arts, the least crafty of crafts. To use a very different metaphor, it is like a baby crying. No instruction is needed. No forethought is required. Need and expression are connected. 'Let my cry come before you', said the Psalmist (Psalm 119.169). Whatever else prayer is, it is rarely the controlled and controlling use of disembodied language.

True prayer is the poetry of the Spirit.

Barefoot praying

Prayer is what happens when humility meets grace, or rather, when humility is met by grace. People today shy away from the virtue of humility for fear that to get close to it will make them weak in the face of hostile others, or in the fear that thinking themselves humble, they might slip into pride. Yet humility is the least negotiable of the Christian virtues. It is the basis of spirituality, wisdom and ministry.[7]

Like many virtues, humility has two opposites. True humility is found midway on the spectrum that begins in self-loathing and ends in arrogance. It is self-acceptance without self-obsession, self-awareness without self-regard. It is no friend of either self-congratulation or self-pity. Humility is a calm and calming virtue, and necessary for the kind of practical attentiveness we call *poise*.

Spiritual traditions and the guides who interpret them are often concerned with the question of *posture*. For those locked into a form of spirituality that is, in essence, a kind of gnosticism (an excessive concern with knowing things or thinking) or emotivism (a disproportionate emphasis on feelings and moods), posture is an unlikely aspect of spirituality. It is much the same for people caught in the web of individualist consumerism (the assumption that what is most important about me is my own individuality and personal gratification together with my self-understood strengths, aptitudes and preferences). For gnostics, emotivists and consumers, the question of posture is irrelevant because posture is of the body, and prayer is all in the mind.

Rather than being irrelevant to spirituality, however, posture is a form of spirituality. This does not mean that you cannot pray apart from certain postures. Some are impossible for some people and there is definitely nothing magic about any particular configuration of arms and legs. Personally I feel that the invitation to prayer which begins with the invitation to bow the head is not always satisfactory. Nor is the instruction to children, 'hands together, eyes closed', quite good enough. But these are quibbles with the way in which people are invited into prayer, not with the fundamental point that bodily posture is a spiritual issue.

Kneeling is a posture of prayer, and so is sitting on the floor, as is standing, as is opening the palms or raising the hands. Pilgrimage is prayer in motion, but it is one thing to go on a journey and another to say it is a pilgrimage. There is an amusing scene in the film *The Way* about the Camino to Santiago de Compostela where the practices of a true or authentic pilgrim are discussed. The absurdity of being too macho about this is brought to light and the question is left unanswered. The reality, however, is that there *is* a difference between a trip and a visit, a pilgrimage and a journey, just as there is a difference between having a relaxing snooze in a comfy chair and spending time in silent prayer. Either may be needed, and I certainly like the first; there can be graceful receptivity in many leisurely activities. But to call it all prayer is to risk sliding into a spiritual life that is all about me being cosied by the Spirit on my own terms. This is the most common spiritual mistake of people who live in a consumer society.

Prayer and pilgrimage involve two potentially uncomfortable components of humility: vulnerability and openness to learning and therefore change. The bow of the head, like the bending of the knee, is intended to reflect and encourage that self-forgetful presence and absorption which sincere and deep prayer requires.

'Prayer is a physically intimate matter',[8] observes Rowan Williams when reflecting on the way Etty Hillesum, the Dutch Jewish writer who perished in Auschwitz, engages with the business of learning how to kneel in her diaries. Although it is a theme to which she repeatedly returns, it is not an easy one for her to dwell on. As Williams observes, she finds it more embarrassing to write about her prayer life than her love life. Maybe that would be true of many of us. We sense that true prayer exposes our deepest being, our soul, and makes us vulnerable. Our prayer is an expression of our integrity.

We fear, I think, that prayer confronts us with what Hannah Arendt once called 'the predicament of irreversibility' in an acute form.[9] Once we have prayed something – in words or groans, gestures or sustained silence – then that is it: there is no unsaying a prayer, whether it is a shout of praise, a cry of lament or a long silent attentiveness to the possibility of grace. We may grow in prayer, learn to pray in ways we feel are rather better, but we know that fundamentally a prayer is a prayer is a prayer: there is no hierarchy. Indeed, you could say that our soul is the sum of all the prayers we have ever said. It's certainly not the edited highlights. It's the lot. Our prayer defines us before God – though mercifully, God always knows us yet more deeply than that. And that's fine. When we pray we throw ourselves on God's mercy. What's awkward about it is what others might make of it all, what others might make of our prayer. Of course, that doesn't *really* matter. Nonetheless it actually does matter. We are human beings, after all. And it is in order to emphasize the down-to-earth *humanness* of our spirituality that I use the metaphor of being barefoot. It doesn't mean getting cold toes: it means being as real as we can.

From the inside, prayer feels like vulnerability and it stretches our capacity to trust. From the outside it can be sublime. To witness acts of prayer is a joy. To see a group of people singing spiritual songs is a delight. To behold a person silently present to grace in a posture of prayer is a very beautiful sight. It is an embodiment of vulnerable and trusting humility such as is depicted in many paintings of the Annunciation. This is the kind of humility that leads to openness, response and trans-formation. It is the kind of humility that lies behind genuine self-giving. It is the inalienable humility of genuine prayer: the most powerful force known to humanity.

This is one of the paradoxes of prayer, which is at once a paradox of Christianity: when we are at our most vulnerable, we are also at our most powerful.

When the silence stops

Let me come clean. This collection of prayers, some of which are more poetic than others, was not written for Lent. It was not written for publication. It was not even written as a collection. And yet there is a common theme.

Each meditation here was written when the silence stopped.

At their best, words are a testimony to what silence cannot achieve. At their worst, words are used as a defence against the threat of silence. In the middle ground, words might point into silence, or lend meaning to that which is as yet meaningless.

A string of events happens. We narrate it. We have a story – a triumph of sorts, a triumph over chaos. We witness something. We describe it. We have a version which others can correct, contradict or improve – another triumph, a triumph of meaning. We experience something within. We coin a metaphor. Someone overhears. They connect it with their own inner world. There is a little bonding, a little fellowship, some misunderstanding too, of course, but also the beginning of spiritual community. Yet another triumph, a victory even: we have both meaning and community.

I wrote the first of these meditations in my little notebook – a friend had given it to me and said, 'It's not for work. It's for creativity only . . .'. As you can imagine, it had remained blank for months. Then, once my courage had built itself up a bit, I began to scribble things in it. In time, I developed the habit of scribbling the first things that came into my head after a time of meditative silence.

Reading them through again later, I would change words and rewrite whole lines. And delete too; yes, there was lots of deleting. I quite liked what was coming into shape on the page then, but the scribble-filled pages were painful to behold and troublesome to decipher. So I typed them up. I still liked them and passed a few of them to some friends. The response was arresting and immediate. I looked again at what I had written and found it was speaking freshly to me. It was through and because of this process that I offered them for publication, though scarcely expecting a Lenten connection.

So what are these strings of words, these verbal meditations, that are called, for want of better words, *Barefoot Prayers*? Mostly they are indeed, directly or indirectly, *prayers*. That is, they are from the heart and yet look beyond themselves to a source of love way outside the self and yet connected to it by a filament of transcending grace. When they are addressed, it is often to 'Thou' or 'Abba', words that I find more helpful in prayer than 'God' or 'Lord'.

Some are perhaps best styled poem-prayers. It feels a slightly turgid description and yet as I have deliberately adopted aspects of a poetic idiom in them it feels honest. It is tiresome to detail too precisely in prose what aspects of the poetic I have used, but let me refer to a loosening of the demands of rationality, a heightening of attention to sound, a reliance on layout and repetition. There is also, I suppose, the hope or belief that if these don't work on the page they might work better when spoken, if for no other reason than that speaking slows things down to the pace of the breath and the tongue. These are not words that run or gallop, though occasionally they begin to canter. They walk. They stumble. They crawl. Sometimes they stop altogether.

One of the high points in the pre-publication gestation of this collection came when I spent an afternoon with the nuns and oblates of Stanbrook Abbey. We sat around in a circle in their calefactory (or 'warmed sitting room') as different people read different prayers. The whole thing was interspersed with music and, of course, silence. It was an intensely moving and humbling experience for me. The readers brought the words to life so gently, freighting what had once been my words with their experience and accent, their hesitations and emphases. The words took flight from various lips and I was convinced that they were no longer my own scribblings but collections of letters and sounds that, by being read and spoken, could allow others a moment of spiritual expression or articulate a spiritual longing or yearning.

* * *

An early reader suggested that I might think of some of these prayers and meditations as 'prayer-stems', a reference to 'story-stems' that are sometimes used to help children begin to narrate their lives. She took as an example the one called 'Simplicity'. Her point was partly that the narrative drive of what I had written was too fast and too direct for her. She needed time to open up the space within and to explore some of the ideas on their own terms before moving on.

This is my version:

> Take from me the desire to accumulate or hoard
> and give me in return a decluttered life
> and simple spirit.
>
> Help me to be content with what is
> and with who I am.
> Help me to delight in what I see,
> what I hear.
> Help me to appreciate the people I know well.
> Help me to see the stranger's grace.

She expands and humanizes this by adding the words shown in italics:

> Take from me the desire to accumulate or hoard.
> *Sometimes I do it because of being worried about running*
>   *out of things.*
> *And sometimes it is just a case of greed – especially when*
>   *it comes to hoarding books.*
> *It is hard for me to pray for an end of my desire to hoard*
>   *books. I am hoping that if I open myself up to this*
>   *possibility, that you won't actually demand it of me.*
>
> Give me a decluttered life and simple spirit.
> *With so much stuff out of the way, I might be able to be*
>   *content with what is and who I am.*

I might even be able to understand who I am.
That would be a start.

Help me to delight in what I see, what I hear.
Help me to appreciate the people I know well. *Sharpen*
    my senses so that I can break through the dull patina
    of familiarity and routine – and really see them, really
    connect with them.
Help me to see the stranger's grace, *and to let myself*
    be seen.

To use a metaphor that I develop in the collection, some of the
prayers here are *monochrome*. They are deliberately grey and
seek to prompt the desire in the reader to colour them in with
honesty.

* * *

Arranging these prayers for Lent and Easter has been a joyful
way to re-encounter them. It has also been surprisingly easy,
and for me a source of unexpected delight as a new counter-
point is set up between a particular prayer and the mood of a
particular day. The Good Friday prayer chose itself, but Holy
Saturday and Easter Day were suggested by the editor, and are,
I think, inspired and creative matches. Only a few prayers were
written for specific days: the Sunday before Lent, Shrove Tuesday
and Palm Sunday.

The project of the book has called for introductions to each
week. I hope these help orient the reader to the pulse of the
Easter journey and the shape of praying represented here, with
its narrative of gathering and then awakening, moving on
through some of life's occasions and puzzles to encounter the
ethical claims of, and the aspiration to, personal virtue – before
coming to the transcending of our mortal and spiritual horizons
in the mystery of Easter newness and victory. Thus we move

from dust to joy, and from the wilderness of temptation to the Promised Land, where our song is 'Alleluia' and the first and last word is 'Amen'.

Notes

1 'The day Thou gavest, Lord, is ended.'
2 P. Tillich, *Shaking of the Foundations* (Harmondsworth: Penguin, 1962), p. 163.
3 W. Brueggemann, *Hopeful Imagination* (Philadelphia: Fortress Press, 1986), p. 25: 'I am increasingly convinced by Paul Ricoeur that people are changed not by ethical urging but by transformed imagination.'
4 R. Llewelyn, *With Pity Not With Blame* (London: Darton, Longman and Todd, 1982), p. 107.
5 Maslow first presented his theory, which has been represented and summarized many times by many other authors, in a paper in the *Psychological Review* in 1943. A. H. Maslow, 'A Theory of Human Motivation', *Psychological Review* 50 (1943).
6 R. M. Rilke, *Letters to a Young Poet*, ed. and trans. M. D. Herter Norton (New York: W. W. Norton, 2004; translation originally copyright 1934), p. 39.
7 In my book *Barefoot Disciple: Walking the Way of Passionate Humility* (London: Continuum, 2010) I developed the idea of barefoot discipleship. The core ideas are reflected in this collection and mentioned through this section. They are that humility is the virtue of down-to-earth connectedness and radical openness which is both authentically Christian and essential for the ongoing learning that is at the heart of living discipleship.
8 R. Williams, *Faith in the Public Square* (London: Bloomsbury, 2012), p. 315.
9 H. Arendt, *The Human Condition* (Chicago: University of Chicago Press, 1958), p. 241.

Week 1

GATHERINGS

———◆·◆·◆———

This collection begins on the Sunday before Lent. Lent is itself a season of preparation, but even preparation can benefit from preparation. Shrove Tuesday is the focus of this, and can helpfully take the form of a day of clearing out and carnival. It begins on a Sunday, partly to honour the resurrection from the start. After all, every Sunday is a little Easter, and Lent is not about forgetting the resurrection. Far from it: without knowing that Lent is a journey to resurrection, Lent can become a sad and sorry time. And in parallel with that my intention is to let love have the first word. The traditional collect for the Sunday Before Lent focuses on the necessity of *charity* in the Christian journey, echoing the famous passage in Paul's first letter to the Corinthians: without love, 'I am a noisy gong or a clanging symbol' (1 Corinthians 13.1). The idea is that love provides the prism through which the whole Lenten journey is seen and imagined.

The week that begins Lent is a strange land of awakening. Shrove Tuesday invites us to turn a corner, to gather up the goodies in the larder, toss a pancake, and revel in Mardi Gras, as we expect and await the austerity of Ash Wednesday. There, a smudge on the forehead brings us down to earth. 'Remember that you are dust and to dust you will return.' That's enough of a thought. But humble mortality alone is not adequate. Nor is plodding on in the same old way. We are to change, turn, repent: 'Turn from sin and be faithful to Christ.' First of all, though, we need to name and pray for the supreme gift: the gift of love.

Sunday

Love

As I set my sights on your
empty tomb,
as I begin to imagine the dangerous route of
desert and temptation,
fasting and fear,
loneliness and crowds,
silence and noise,
desertion and betrayal,
bread and wine,
cross and nails,
vinegar and gall,
water and blood,
spice and earth,
cave and rock . . .
as I imagine and foresee all this,
and stoop not to tie but to
unlace my boots,
take off my shoes,
slip off my sandals . . .
I pray for just one thing:
your gift of love.

Worthless the effort,
worthless the strain,

worthless the travel,
worthless the cross,
without your love.

So give me, I pray,
the love that heals,
the love that forgives,
the love that longs to be given
away.

Give me the love that grows,
that I may grow in love,
in love, in love,
in love.

Monday

Fullness of Life

Give me, this day,
a lung full of spirit,
an eye full of beauty,
a step full of joy,
a mouth full of praise,
and hands full of nothing
but desire to do your will.

Shrove Tuesday

—————••••—————

Feast

I go to the store cupboard
looking for eggs and
memories.
They need to be broken and
beaten,
blended with flour,
left to stand.

I heat a pan, hot,
very hot.
The batter spreads thin
and quickly browns
at the edges.
Choosing the moment I
make my move:
toss it, flip it, turn it over,
deftly.

A few more seconds
and it is done.
Sugared and soured, it is
ready for the feast . . .

that initiates the fast.
The long, slow,
rambling fast, the
wilderness fast,
the map-less fast where no
recollection can find the way ahead.

All the more reason, then, to
travel light
to leave my bags
at the station,
to lose my property,
to empty the pantry of its
tinned regrets, its
bottled remorse, its
mildewed mass of mistakes.

No point curating this lot,
or carting it about any more.
Let me throw it all away,
deftly.

Ash Wednesday

Repentance

Walking into the ocean
the cold bites toes and ankles.
Sand is ripped from footprint
in the ebb and flow of surf
even at an inch's depth.
Pushing on, each wave becomes a body blow, a
thud on the belly
a crash on the chest.
The eighth, the biggest, pushes me
back a pace or two.
Best to lunge over or
dive under, through
water, suspended sand and murky foam.

This is what it is to face
the One who was and is and is to come.
This is what it is to face the Creator
who comes in Spirit and storm.

Yet:

if this is what it is to face,
maybe I am facing wrongly.
In the surf there is no
question. The journey out allows the return;
what seemed like infinite
resistance, is now propelling power.

Let me turn my back,
not in disrespect, but in true alignment;
and speed me along the new forward,
my old backward.

Thursday

Breath of God

Breath of God,
be my life this day;
be my compassion.

Breath of God,
be my connection with your
places of distress and darkness;
with your places of despair and desolation.

Breath of God,
flow where you are not expected;
flow where there is hurt and hatred.

Breath of God,
flow where life is coming to an end;
flow into the kingdom of death.

Breath of God,
flow into me, through me, from me:
as grace, as love, as Spirit, as life.

Breath of God, breath of God, breath of God,
breathe on me,
breathe with me

breathe me.

Friday

Bread

Abba Jesus,
you ask me to follow.
Let me follow you as bread.

Knead me and rest me.
Raise me, bake me and
break me.
Set me at the centre
    and disperse me.

Let me be absorbed by others
    multiplied in their hearts.
Let me be collected as manna
    or as leftovers.
Let me be in twelve baskets
    when your work is done.

You are the bread of life.
I trust you to feed me with a
fragment;
to fill me with the smallest
crumb.

Saturday

Hospitality

Never take from us that vaguely anxious
curiosity we feel when we
behold a new face,
hear a new name,
when we give attention to someone unknown.

Give us keen interest
in whatever stories and storms lie
within the one who is new to us, and
let that interest become respect,
and the respect flower as
reverence.

Let us bow before whatever triumphs and wounds,
hurts and guilts,
mistakes, misadventures and madnesses
make this stranger unknown and yet knowable,
unlikely yet likeable.

O Christ! Many found you to be strange,
and yet the most vulnerable found healing and
peace in your presence.
Make friends of us
that we might be ready friends to strangers
as strange as ourselves.

Week 2

AWAKENINGS

————◆•◆•◆————

To make the transition from sleep is to walk slowly to a new spiritual space. It takes time to wake up, and the time can be filled with longing, adventure and discovery.

The dawning of a new day is a powerful metaphor for renewal, refreshment, hope and continuity. Dawn is a time of prayer for all who connect their praying with the movements of the spheres – as so many do, both individuals and traditions.

Who can fail to be touched and renewed when they take the time to sit at a window, or in the open air, and watch the dawn happen? To rest while the earth turns, the stars disappear, the sky becomes milky, then rose, then blue. To witness the dawn is to connect not just with the earth but with the universe. No wonder the Christian faith points and draws us to the dawn of dawns, the rising of the light that scatters all darkness.

To witness the dawn is to relive resurrection.

It is not like that every day. Many days begin without our observation, because our attention is elsewhere: on our tasks, on our lists of things to do, on our worries, on our dread that the day will be stressful – or, worse – dull beyond words.

A down-to-earth spirituality of awakening, of entering into a new day, will have elements of both. Every day is special, and every day is ordinary too.

Sunday

Awakening

As the sun brightens the sky,
revealing the greens of the day,
touching the clouds with pink,
beckoning the birds to their wings
and ourselves to work . . .
Let our hearts rise within us.
Let our bodies unwind for activity.
Let our wills be trained to your purpose.

Let our dreams form our minds
and our minds sift our dreams.

Help us to be your servants this day.
To do your will and walk your way
with humility, care and true,
true, joy.

Monday

Psalm of the Dawn

As the sun climbs above the hill, to show itself in blinding
light and warming heat; so you appear in our heart after
the long night of darkness.

In darkness I have slept, and in the cold shivered; I know
my ignorance and fear, I am alone in the cosmos.

Before the dawn the birds were roused; calling to wake the
earth, singing hope, insisting on the coming of day.

I heard them not; I rested long in my fear. I trembled to be alone.

The stars returned to their place, invisible beyond the
heavens; driven back by the coming of the sun.

The beasts retired to their lairs; their fear was of the dawning
day, to be exposed by the coming of the light.

Within the plants sap began to flow; the first light of dawn
touching the green to life.

With the full light of sun the green is bright; the air cleaned
by the growing.

How happy are they who see the dawn; those for whom
night is gone.

How happy are they who feel the warmth of the sun; those
who know its strength will sing.

How happy are they who greet the day, with faith and health restored; they will do your will.

Dawning God, dispel all the thoughts and fears of night, and give us, with your creation, refreshment and renewal, that we might this day reflect your light into the lives of others.

Tuesday

Important Commission

Let this day be calm and confident
because I have an important
commission. I need to do my best
for others without anxiety, rush or panic.
Keep me focused.
Keep me open-minded.
Keep me in mind.
Remain in my thoughts, close to my
pulse.

Let me breathe deeply.
Let me enjoy each moment as it passes
and hold me back when I begin
to try to do, or say, or achieve too much.

May today be a good day.

Wednesday

To Do List

I don't yet have a list.
Only the prospect of a list.
An orderly, linear a, b, c
of what I must.

I have items
jangling in my mind,
swirling and arching,
each with different dread,
every one with the potential to expand –
to explode into a day's work.

I resist the idea of making a
list of items. Why cage them or make them tame?
I like their colourful, darting
behaviour, hide and
seek across the cortex.
'Oh, I had forgotten that.
Must remember to do it after lunch.'

Give me a net and the skill to
use it to trap those darting-fish thoughts,
those important tasks to be done.

Help me to land them, sort them,
work my way through them.

Help me to focus my attention, my
time, my energy where it can
be most effective.

And let me throw the little fish back;
let me catch them another
day – when they have grown.

Thursday

May This Day Be Blessed

'May this day be blessed.'
I do not know what that means
in advance.

I am asking for happiness,
but not for anything superficial.

'May this day be blessed.'
I hope it will be indeed.
But how?

I am asking for a visit of grace,
but not for anything disruptive.

'May this day be blessed.'
If it is, it will not be by my effort,
but by my acceptance.

I am asking for openness,
the capacity to receive.

'May this day be blessed.'
As was yesterday,
though I am not sure how.

Let my eye see backwards
and notice the blessing that was.

'May this day be blessed.'
I am confident that it will be.

My prayer is not for anything more,
simply to see and feel and know.

'May this day be blessed.'
Not in the anticipation but
in the living.

'May this day be blessed.'
Not by what I give or receive,
but in what I see and feel.

'May this day be blessed.'
And may I be part of the blessing.

Friday

The Day Looks Dull

The day is planned.
Its priorities established.
The diary, like a section through a landscape,
has been built up over time.
Layers laid down.
But that does not make it
interesting,
exciting
or in any way promising.

To be frank, this day looks dull.
The diary looks too full.
I wish there were more gaps.
A little white space for creativity,
or recreation, perhaps.

So my prayer is serious.
I need a lifeline of spirit;
an injection of hope.
I need to see the possible in the
predictable.
I need to see the space in the congestions.
I need to see again the
humanity of the people I will spend
the day with; the spirituality of those
I encounter across the meeting table.

Refurnish me with a sense of
purpose for these all-so-slowly-burning
projects and
quietly unfolding plans.
Replenish me with vision.
Renew me with hope of
transformative action.
Rekindle in me the passion that long since
got me involved in all this.
Rouse my sense of responsibility for
my time, and rid me of the
fantasy that a day in your service
could be dull.

The day is planned. Nonetheless, let it be
    unpredictable.

Saturday

Litany for a New Day

That we may be given the prudence to seek your truth,
   however uncomfortable or unsettling.
Lord of the dawn: **Shine on your world.**

That we may be given the courage to work for economic
   and social justice.
Lord of the dawn: **Shine on your world.**

That we may be given the wisdom to seek your kingdom
   before all else.
Lord of the dawn: **Shine on your world.**

That we may be given the faith to follow wherever you
   call us.
Lord of the dawn: **Shine on your world.**

That we may be given the hope to see beyond the troubles
   of today.
Lord of the dawn: **Shine on your world.**

That we may be given the constancy to endure all kinds
   of trials and tribulations for the sake of your gospel.
Lord of the dawn: **Shine on your world.**

That we may be given the love which makes us credible
   advocates of your will and purpose.
Lord of the dawn: **Shine on your world.**

That we may be given the patience to wait for your final coming in glory.
Lord of the dawn: **Shine on your world.**

That we may be given the vision to glimpse your glory and to see signs of your love.
Lord of the dawn: **Shine on your world.**

Week 3

OCCASIONS

———•◆•———

Prayer is often connected to occasions, whether they are special occasions or rites of passage. There is a deep intuition behind this and it helps us to find direction and draw the whole of ourselves – mind, body and spirit – into the moments, hours and days that matter most because so much is focused on them.

These prayers concern entering more deeply into the moment, into the limited time of opportunity, whether on a daily basis – a tea or coffee break – or on days of special significance: when we move house, when we find ourselves speaking to others, or when to our surprised delight things have been good and we have done well.

The point about an occasion is that it is passing. These prayers are intended to grace certain occasions (though when read as part of this Lenten sequence they will be working retrospectively, whether by the power of memory or proleptically – looking forward to the next speaker day or listening day).

This gracing is not intended to fix or limit. These prayers are not holes in the ground in which to bury the treasure of a passing moment, nor are they a shelter, home or temple.

Yet by adding words of prayer to an occasion and drawing the reality – often confused – into prayerful meditation, life's moments can be touched and transfigured: not becoming something else or something permanent, but becoming, yet more fully and deeply, their fleeting, phosphorescent self.

Sunday

On Receiving Thanks

I am beside myself with delight.
But also feeling awkward and embarrassed.
I was not expecting this,
though it is not entirely undeserved.
I have been thanked this day
sincerely, appropriately,
unnecessarily.
So the thanks came as a surprise
and I am chuffed to bits.
What do I say now?

Thou, Great God, Thou art the ultimate recipient of thanks,
Thou, Holy One, receive praise without end.
Can you know the impact of simple, unaffected gratitude
on an insecure, flagging spirit like mine?
Can you understand that this causes not only delight
but problem?

I want to push it back.
To shake it off.
To negative the positive.
To make it neutral: 'it was nothing';
'your thanks is nothing'.

But neither were nothing.
I have been thanked for my effort and
skill, diligence and care.
I am thrilled.
Yet still, I am cautious, in case
in thrilling something is spoilt
or lost.

My soul wants to sing.
Let it sing!
It sings praise to the God who
created praise.
It sings thanks to Thou,
creator of thanks.
I thank Thou,
truly thank-worthy One,
for all who have ever surprised me
with their thanks.
Recent thank-ers.
Surprising thank-ers.
Those whose thanks came from a crisis.
Chronic thank-ers.
Subtle thank-ers.
Overstated, balloon-like thank-ers.
Thanking strangers, thanking friends.
I give thanks for them all,
and pray for the generosity of spirit and
imagination to be sincere, convincing
and joyful
as I give thanks myself.

Monday

Coffee Break

This is not a special occasion.
There is no form, no dress-code.
Nothing seems at stake, though
I know it is.

This is not a real time.
More a break, a gap,
an interval, an interlude, perhaps.
A grown-up's vestige of
playtime.

Yet it is as real and sacred as
any meal,
as worthy of grace.

As the coffee flows from the
pot, or takes form in the cup,
I pray a blessing on those
who grew the beans, milked
the cows; on those who transported it all
to me.

I am in a shop. I pray for the staff:
keep them cheerful and give them
good leisure when their work is done. I
pray that their wages are fair.

I am at work. I pray for my
colleagues and workmates: give
them interesting and wholesome
tasks and help us get on.

I am at home. I pray for
this place and those I share it with:
may good things happen
under our roof.

I am visiting others. I pray for
those giving me hospitality, whether
I was invited or just dropped in:
may our conversation be
honest, kind-hearted and rich.

I am alone. I pray for good
thoughts. Let me take a minute
or two of calm, of silence.
Let my imagination, my
mind, my heart commune; let
them make peace together.

May this moment be refreshing;
    a time of real progressing;
        a rich and real blessing;
            a daily cup of peace.

Tuesday

Listening Day

Lord, let this be a listening day.
Let me be attentive.

Start me with silence.

Let me put my ear to the breeze,
the sky, the hum of traffic, the distant work.

Let me connect with birdsong, irritating insect buzz,
with school playground in the distance,
river under bridge, rain on glass.

Let me read the off-stage sounds.
Let my mind follow my ear.

Help me use the 'off-switch'.
Ration my exposure to noise.

When I am listening to others, let me
use my eyes, my heart.
Let me hear tone of voice, inflection,
hesitation.
Give me the calm that winkles the
stammering thought from the frightened tongue.

When music comes, let me
enter into its texture, its depth.
When there is singing, let me hear the soul.
If there is applause, open me to its energy, delight and warmth.

When reading, slow me down, on screen
or page, from book or report.
Let me imagine the writer, in haste or in deep thought;
   rushing
it off or editing carefully and with sorrow.
Give me some sense of what lies
behind the passage I see.
Let my eyes read between the lines,
around the words, above
and below the paragraphs.

Return me to silence again.
Let me hear my footsteps, my
heartbeat, my breathing.
Let me hear your Spirit
as it broods over all.

Wednesday

Speaking Day

It's my turn to speak today.
And I am certain of two things.
That I will feel underprepared.
That I will be inclined to say too much.

Moderate my anxieties.
Consolidate my thoughts.
Calm my mind and let
the words come along in an orderly but not entirely
predictable fashion.

Spare them my more banal, self-indulgent,
flippant or half-baked thoughts.
Keep me from rant, cant and claptrap.

Let my words be authentic and true,
heartfelt and clear.
Let them be like opening curtains,
clearing mist, ripening fruit,
refreshing rain.
Let them be the cause of someone else's
flourishing.

Thursday

Moving House

Over the years, it has all become
so familiar. I painted the walls,
put up the shelves. We chose curtains together
and carpets. Every room has seen
domestic drama.
I've been unwell here and recovered again.
I've read and worked.
I've praised and sworn,
known energy and exhaustion and
all states in between.

The food we've eaten – Oh!
The friends entertained – Oh!
The laughs – Ha!
The struggles and disputes – Oh! Oh!

The hurt, the harm, the forgiveness – Yes!
The offence, grief and reconciliation – Yes!

All this in these walls,
under this roof,
in this space.

I have called it home.

As I prepare to leave, to allow
my body to be relocated for a while,
I try a prayer.
But to whom?
Son of Man had nowhere to lay his head.
Son of Man cannot understand the deep
soul-security of home that I know
I will grieve.
What can the wandering prophet know of the
everyday solidarity of ordinary stuff,
the loved and ignored
twigs of my nest.

So I cast my prayer beyond,
fling it to Thou, Abba,
creator of habitat and home,
member of family,
giver of land,
inspiration for all solidarity,
faithfulness,
constancy.

My prayer is raw.
'I want to stay!
Just let me abide
one more day.

'Let my eye rest on the faded paint,
the stained carpet,
the accumulated junk, each
object a story, a novel without
a cover, or title, written in my mind.

'Oh let me stay in my home!
Be rid of my comforters and cajolers.
This is my home! There
is no other.

'Allow me that loyalty at least. My
memory has gone. I am
empty within. Let me see my past.
Hide from me my future.

'Lord, let me not know my end.

'Let me stay!

'But when I go
abide Thou with me.'

Friday

―――・●・―――

After a Holiday

I had my hopes and they were high.
My expectations were not specific:
they were about wellbeing and
contentment; pleasure enjoyable enough
to be remembered.
I had expectations of peaceful hours,
delightful scenes, pleasing encounters.
A change of pace was needed –
I removed my watch – let the sun
tell the time.

Now the watch is back on my wrist.
The time of holiday comes to its end. In this
interim, travel-back time, let me take a flight
of gratitude.

And so I give thanks:
for opportunity,
for time,
for the efforts of others,
for companions,
for encounters,
for everything that delighted
the eye,
for each moment of peace,
for inspiration from art and nature,

for the cool of morning,
for the warm of evening,
for food and drink,
for laughter and smiles,
for safe travel,
for a home to return to.
Alleluia.
Amen.

Saturday

Evensong

As the sunlight loses its strength,
and the shadows stretch to the east,
so our weary minds seek rest.

We wish the day had been longer,
that we might have given more
where less had not been enough.

We long to have another chance to do
the same again, without mistake,
without hesitation or lack of conviction.

Our day seems pallid, pale and underused;
opportunity became apparent only too late.
The moment passed too quickly for us;
once again we were too dull.

We look forward to a rest of depth,
a still and noiseless vacancy.
We fear, yet hope for a revealing dream
but dread the nightmare that accuses and alarms.

Give us, we pray, our daily rest,
that we might live tomorrow better than today.
But teach us, first, to say that while not perfect,
this day was, in the end, okay.

Week 4

PUZZLES

Life raises questions. It creates predicaments. It leads to situations that are not easily resolved and conflicts that refuse to be reconciled. Life is full of puzzles: and our prayer should embrace and hold some of the puzzles that we experience.

In this section, a few of life's puzzles are presented and explored. The fact of our bodiliness, the reality of loneliness, the truth that we know as disappointment, the realization that some things, no matter how much we wish they might begin to appear beautiful to us, remain unlovely: these are the human realities we bring into the calm and loving spaciousness of prayer.

The most challenging two puzzles presented here are, perhaps, *emptiness* and *hatred*. These are awkward, uncomfortable, embarrassing states. We wish that the words were alien to us, that we really had no idea what they meant. The truth, however, is that we are all too well acquainted with these realities. What happens, though, when we draw them kicking and screaming into prayer? There is no answer. Sometimes it is a softening. Sometimes it is an intensification leading to an explosion and then resolution. A different path of prayer has been set out in each case. Your own may be similar or different, but whatever the detail, when puzzle meets prayer some grace is liberated: something very new transpires.

Puzzle plus prayer makes for new creation. Maybe that's the point of the puzzle.

Sunday

Mindful

I am mindful of my own chatter,
mental chatter,
clutter and detritus.
But good stuff too.

I sift it,
shaking the sieve gently.
There is so much to remove,
so much not worth dwelling on.

I see what remains in the sieve.
The very stuff I want to forget.
It draws me in.
Compels my attention, raises a question,
invites an emotional response.

I let it lie there:
a heap of broken toys,
a pile of garden refuse,
yesterday's tealeaves,
tomorrow's compost,
today's distraction.

Today's treasure:
that is something else.
It has been sifted out
and lies, hidden, below.

Who would have thought it so
friable,
so lacking in volume,
so indifferent in colour and texture.

It is dust.
Let me be mindful of mental dust.

Monday

Bodies

Thank you, Abba, for the gift we know most intimately but
  fear most profoundly:
our body of flesh and blood.
Thank you for the experiences and desires that animate our
  bodily life,
for our appetites and needs
and also for our vulnerabilities and sensitivities.

We hold before you both the delights and the frights which
our bodily nature has given us over the years.
We thank you for such bodily grace as is ours,
in repose or inaction,
in form or activity.

We praise you for the charm and pleasure,
threat and wonder,
of youthful growth.
We ask your companionship as we face the
fears that ageing brings.

We crave your courage whenever disease catches us unawares,
whenever we feel pain,
whenever our bodies let us down.

Hear us as we pray for those whose bodies are like ours in
    some ways.
Family members we resemble,
people with similar gifts and aptitudes,
those with similar disabilities, disorders or restrictions;
those who endure the same regimes to keep them healthy.

Give us a sense of unity, security and fellowship that
    strengthens us all
and enriches each individual character.

Abba – you have made us bodily; give us bodily grace.

Tuesday

Loneliness

I feel it come at unexpected times; that sense of not
belonging
that hijacks my confidence,
cracks my control,
warps my wellbeing.

Anything can set it off.
Time alone.
Crowds.
A phone call that ends abruptly.
A letter that never arrives.
Seeing a group of people happy together.
The celebrations of others.
Seeing a soul lost inside itself in confusion or pain or
    boredom – and
thinking 'that too is me'.
Even the mirror can make me lonely.
The real mirror or the reflective state of mind.
Mistakes, regrets, guilt – all these cut me off.
Shame too. That seals it.
Embarrassment, oddly, does not work like that. It makes an
    awkward
connection. The blush is never lonely.
Loneliness has pale cheeks and sad, still eyes that look down.
Loneliness knows the look of the earth, the pavement, the path,
the road, the field, the floor – carpeted, wood or stone.

So here is my prayer to you,
Three in one.
You!
One in three.
You!
Who are always in company.
Come, accept, respect, honour the loneliness that I know
but cannot share.
Come drink of the cup.
Not the cup of company or communion.
Come drink the cup of sorrow!
Drink it alone and to the dregs!
Drink it as I have done;
when my companions sleep;
when the tormentors torment;
when the mockers mock!

Drink the bitter gall of loneliness
extended on a sponge!
Drink loneliness with me and I will never be alone again!

And let me remember your drinking,
even when lost in my
self.

Wednesday

Emptiness

Abba, patient one,
have mercy on me as I come to you
with nothing to give.
Have mercy on my tired mind.
Have mercy on my empty hands.
Have mercy on my weary legs.
Have mercy on a heart that feels like a vacuum.

Abba, patient one,
in the absence of anything to give, I
pray for the blessing of your grace.
I do not ask to be fulfilled.
I do not ask for a burst of energy.
I do not ask for a vision.
I could not bear sudden enthusiasm – so
spare me that.

Abba, patient one, bless my lack of gift.
Bless my tired mind.
Bless my empty hands.
Bless my weary legs.
Bless my inner vacuum.

Abba, patient one, give me the patience to wait
on your blessing.
Give me the patience to wait on your grace.
Give me patience enough to live
with myself, as myself
but not for myself.
Give me the patience to love
the blessing of inadequacy,
weakness, fatigue and emptiness.
Give me the patience to live
by your grace
at your pace.

Thursday

Hatred

Sometimes it happens.
I respond
as I should not.
I react.
I tense up.
I go hot or, maybe,
cold.

When I have seen carelessness or
cruelty or the
abuse of power or
arrogance in action
and I have seen people hurt.
People like me.
Even me.

To call it anger is true – but
it is more than anger.
Anger is like an espresso:
bitter, short and with a kick that
enlivens.

This is something stronger. It is
Hatred.
Yes, capital 'H'.
It is a bitter cup, to be sure.
But it is long and its effects are slow.

Hatred.
It has found a home in me.
Wormed its way through my better self
and into my soul to lay its poisonous
parasitical spawn.

I feel it growing.
I feel it gnawing.
I feel it rising within.
It controls my heartbeat.
It sours my countenance.
It grips my voice, making some things
impossible to say;
adding a sneer where a smile is needed.

Deliver me of this pernicious pregnancy
of my person.
Break its grip on my
vitality.
Smash its growing control of
my being.
Deal violently with this hatred of mine.
Turn it against itself.
Let it rant if it must.

Take its force, O Thou,
crucified one.
Take its dark, dark passion.
Take its pain with each damned nail.
Impale it on your tree.
Let the ones I hate go free.
Teach us how to live in Thee.

Friday

Disappointment

Abba, I turn to you without energy,
the light of my eyes has gone,
my strength has fallen from me.

You know where my heart has been.
You know where my hopes were set.
You gave me that vision, that thought,
that dream.

Now it is gone
and without it I am as helpless as can be.
Like an asthmatic child, my spirit
wheezes where once I breathed deeply.
Like an arthritic elder, I cannot
walk as boldly as I used.
I cannot stride. It is as much
as I can do to shuffle.
The thought of dancing is abhorrent to me.
I would rather cry than sing.
If I tried to sing, I would wail.

Steady me, kindly Abba.
Help me not to hate the dream
that now lies shattered, or myself for
dreaming it.
Help me to overcome the shame of having hoped
in vain.

Help me not to rest in this disappointment but to pass
    through it.
Help me to harvest the sad fruits in this garden
not for their sourness but for their strange sweetness.

With you the darkness is always the herald of dawn.
With you true hope is always new.
With you there is always blessing.

Send some kind angel to help
me find the blessing in this.
I cannot see it yet.

Saturday

The Unlovely

Praise God for big black birds,
jackdaws and crows,
rooks and ravens;
unsung and unsinging
they fail to attract our
friendly feelings.

Raise a prayer for all that is unlovely.
Items badly made,
mean materials,
artless assortments.

Offer thanks for
all that is cheap and cheerful,
kitsch or clichéd;
for disposable things;
for things on which our eye never rests;
for stuff always destined to be clutter or junk.

Help us learn to love the unlovely
that we might find ourselves loving
the unlovely in others,
and that the unlovable parts of ourselves
might feel the warmth and worth of true love.

Week 5

RESPONSES

————•◦•————

Our senses are constantly bombarded, and yet we miss most of what happens around us. It goes by us, past us, over our heads. We attend only to a fraction, a tiny fraction, of what we might.

Then something strikes us. We don't know why, but we are paying attention and this thing, event, reality or whatever, begins to matter. This is a blessing: this thing – whatever it is – that is drawing us out of ourselves. It is melting our loneliness and forging some kind of connection, making a pathway for communion.

The prayers in this section are responses to something that has grabbed our attention. Rain, for instance. What do we make of rain? Do we find a way of making it irrelevant by donning waterproofs or going indoors and hiding until it is all over? Or is it part of the mysterious wonder of today, of now? Personally, I always disliked the sound of rain. Too many childhood memories of having to stay indoors or being drenched while outside, perhaps. Then, one spring day, someone told me that its drumming was a kind of music, a dance even, and that I should listen to it.

The daily news is another reality that we might monitor or respond to more fully. The true sadness of news is that its sadness is so overwhelming that we lose the capacity to respond. Maybe we should pray for the spiritual, emotional and intellectual capacity to *hear* the news, and to relate to the suffering of which it speaks.

This responses section is perhaps the most connected with issues of justice, or rather the lack of justice. It is no accident that it comes at the middle of the collection. Justice, or rather the *lack of* justice, or the *longing for* justice, is at the heart of prayer. And prayer is what fuels us to continue to struggle with all the forces and powers, all the sins and weaknesses, including our own, which stand in the way of justice.

This whole collection is based on the simple idea that the core of spirituality is not the quest to achieve, to know or to do anything. It is the anti-quest of seeking *not* to inhibit grace by getting in the way, while remaining fully, really, positively present. At a very deep level, this quest is one and the same as the quest for justice. When we let grace in, justice follows. When we seek justice we follow the prompting of grace. All this is heart work as well as hand work, leg work, brain work and social work. This is why we must pray not only from the rage that sees and feels injustice, but for the heart of connection and compassion, the heart of grace.

Sunday

Doing Justice

The prophet said, 'Do Justice!'
Why did the prophet not say more?
There is too much justice to do.
There is so much justice lacking. The scope for my action is
vast, daunting, infinite.
I not only feel small.
I feel infinitesimally small.
A vanishing point in the endless
expanse of injustice.

The prophet said, 'Do Justice!'
And I cried, 'Which Justice?'
Criminal justice.
Social justice.
Economic justice.
Retributive justice.
Restorative justice.
Generational justice.
I want to do justice to the prophet's words.
I want to do justice to justice.
Where shall I begin?
Oh where shall justice be found
and where is the place of fairness?

Let me go there. I will go there with
humility. For I am not able to travel in
any other way. My only method is plodding,
one step at a time.
One foot on the ground, one swinging forward in a
controlled fall.

Lord God Almighty!
Help me to walk humbly
and let me not walk alone.
And when I come to the crossroads,
when I need to make a decision,
when I have just open wilderness
all around me – incline me and nudge me
towards the place of justice.
Turn me from the place of ambition,
of acquisition, of avarice.
Steer me from the place
of self, of self, of self.
Take me to the place of
respect, restitution, reconciliation.

And take me there *kindly*,
that my footsteps might be
mercy and grace,
mercy and grace,
mercy and grace,
mercy and grace,
mercy and grace,
for ever and ever and ever.
Amen.
Mercy and grace for ever.
Amen.

Monday

On Hearing the News

I am struggling.
I am struggling to hold
what I have heard and seen.

Daily I am assailed by news;
daily I struggle to absorb it, to drink
the cup of other people's suffering.

Teach me how to hear the news;
show me how to respond.

For a while my heart grows hot, my mind
moves on. I am left with feelings
I cannot name.

I am not covered with anger or
roused to rage; my tears are not shed.
I fail in sympathy.

Yet there is a simmering shame,
a vague guilt; not a
sword, but a blunt saw
hacking at my soul.

Let me lament the sorrow I see!
Let me rage at routine injustice!

Let my inner eye run with tears:
when I see the hungry,
when I hear of violent death,
when peace talks fail.

Let my inner eye run with tears:
when I hear of natural disaster,
when I see storm or flood,
when the endangered become extinct.

Let my inner eye run with tears:
when I see corruption,
when I hear of deceit,
when justice cannot be done.

But let my soul sing:
when I hear of courage and creativity;
when I see adversity overcome;
when the story is of sacrifice and service.

Let me attend to the depth of the news.

Let me resonate with the reality it both reveals
and hides.

Tuesday

Rain

As the raindrops drum against the windowpane
and drill on the tiles,
we give thanks for precipitation falling as drizzle
or in storms
to water the earth,
feeding and freshening by day and by night.

We pray for all who live in dry
and drought-affected places;
for people living with dust and desiccation.

We pray for those who are deluged;
we think of those who are constantly damp.
We pray for those in danger of flood or coping with its aftermath.
We pray for those living with the difficulty of frozen water,
    burst pipes,
slippery paths, broken gutters.

We pray for good, wetting, watery rain wherever it is needed
by humankind.
And we pray for the gratitude that informs our
attitude and makes us good stewards of your life-giving,
earth-shaping,
planet-defining,
indispensable gift of water.

We thank you for this day of rain;
let its rhythm help our alleluia to dance.

Wednesday

The Lost

Rarely have I been lost,
seriously lost, unable to find a way forward or a way home.
Often enough I have been a little unsure of
exactly where I am
or a bit bewildered as I consider
whether to turn left or right
or go straight on.

Being truly lost is my genuine nightmare.
I find myself just too confused.
I see no familiar view or place.
I see no friendly face.
I do not understand the words I hear.
I misread the signs.
Notices are a mystery to me.

Many are lost this day.
Too far away from home to return,
alienated from all that is around.
Distant from whatever is closest.
Close only to their own sense of fear
and smallness.

So many of the lost are children.
Rejected by parents unable to love.
Let go by parents unable to cope.
Taken by fleeing parents from violence and famine.
Stolen or kidnapped to be sold or used.

Refugee child, Christ child, hold them in your silent embrace
when they are at their most lost.

So many of the lost are elderly,
unable to remain on good-enough terms with the people
   who populate
their past and shuffle in the corridors of their minds:
straining to see and hear and to accept
the pace of change
that outstrips personal and private decay;
driven by need from homeland and unable to cope
in premature demise;
racked in pain and ailment,
rendered miserable and shunned;
experiencing diminishment of body and
loss of mind, feeling memories slip through
frail and wrinkled fingers.

Ancient of Days, draw them forward to
Thy light
Thy peace
Thy company
Thy home.

Thursday

People With Nowhere to Sit

On a journey we know we need,
sooner or later,
to find somewhere to sit.
It does not matter if the distance is
short, or the time
brief.
Standing will suffice for a little while.
But when we travel a long way, on
a bus or a train,
we need a seat.
And when we walk for hour after hour, mile after mile,
we need, after a while,
and for a while,
a place to sit.

Thank God for sitting places:
familiar seats and chairs,
benches and couches,
boards and steps,
the places we like to be
for rest or work
or company,
where we sit to watch TV
where we often have our tea
where we rest awhile with Thee.

I am grateful for the chance to sit.
The chance to stay.
The chance to pray.
Remembering multitudes who hope for more,
but only ever have the floor.

Bless them as they walk.
Bless them as they squat.
Bless them as they feel the earth.
Bless them as they stand and sway.
Bless all who have no seat, this day.

Friday

Those Who Cry Out

Hear the prayer, O Lord, of all who cry to thee
in their trouble:
those who cry out in hunger;
those who cry out in pain;
those who cry out in fear;
those who cry out in panic;
those who cry out in loneliness;
those who cry out in despair;
those who cry out in grief;
those who cry out from a broken heart;
those who cry out with a wounded voice;
those who cry out with deep foreboding;
those who cry out from bitter memory;
those who cry out to you to forgive because they cannot;
those who cry out to you for their children and who will not
   be comforted;
those who cry out to you by night;
those who cry out to you without ceasing;
those whose cries are stifled for further fear;
those whose cries are inward and unheard.
Hear the prayer, O Lord, of these and all others who cry out,
and pour upon their wounds
the healing balm of your mercy.

Saturday

A Heart of Grace

The more insistent the birdsong,
the more powerful the scent of flowers,
the more majestic the tree
    expansive in its own space
    solid in its own roots
    luxuriant in its own branches, twigs and leaves,
the more active the insects,
the more webs the spider spins –
the more indifferent nature appears.

Rain falls on the just
    and the unjust.
Sun shines on the good and the evil.
Broken leg or arm,
    cracked rib,
    punctured lung,
all mean nothing to the tree
from which I fell.
Heartless is the shattering glass,
    the collapsing wall,
    the quaking earth.
Care-free the blackbirds outside the open window
where the one who cannot sleep for pain
lies lonely in distress.

So make in us a heart that cares:
that sees,
feels,
holds,
bleeds,
breaks and
rages in concert with others.
Make in us a heart that
hurts and
heals, that
shares and
saves the suffering from
the loneliness of natural life.

Take from us the heart of stone,
the heart of flesh.
Give us the heart of
grace.

Week 6

VIRTUES

———◆◆◆———

The prayers in this section reflect the desire to grow in virtue.

I am convinced that while part of our praying is to offer to God the needs of the world, there is at least as great a need to offer to God our own unfinishedness, our far-from-perfectness. It may seem selfish to pray for one's own personal development, but I don't believe it is. It was Gandhi who said that if you wanted to change the world you should start with yourself, and that wisdom is relevant here. The prayer for virtue is one which asks God to give us the quality or strength of character that we need to be a more helpful partner in doing God's will on earth. Anyone with an ounce of self-awareness will know that good work is subverted by our own lack of patience or courage or determination or our limited kindness or generosity or . . . The list of ways in which we undermine our own best efforts is endless.

Prayer for increased grace in these areas is, it seems to me, the flipside of prayers of confession that we have sinned, fallen short, done what we ought not to have done and left undone things we ought to have done. Certainly we need forgiveness for all this, but we also need to be bold enough to put on the table of prayer the petition that we would rather like to be a more healthy and wholesome partner in God's project of transformation, redemption and healing. We may be happy enough to recite the idea that 'there is no health in us', but if we use that health-less-ness as our excuse for making a mess of our own lives and the lives of others, our vision of a good Christian life is somewhat deficient. Seeking forgiveness without seeking to grow in virtue is, I suggest, a form of spiritual complacency.

It might be that the inherited metaphors of absolution have let us down. We think of our spotted slates being wiped clean or our health restored. Better, perhaps, to think of being put back on our feet – and realizing that it is now our own responsibility both to discern the right direction in which to walk and to begin to put one foot in front of another.

Now if that sounds difficult – well, that's why it needs to go into prayer.

Sunday

Patience

This is a big ask, but I dare to ask for patience for myself.
For a sense of the right pace and
the right time.
Help me to develop a deep sense of the way your providence
unfolds, its moments
and its seasons.
Take from me the nervous desire to hasten.

Banish from my lips all unnecessary
talk of urgency or rush.
Remove from my actions all that projects busyness.
Help me to be prompt and punctual without rushing,
and to know when to move on when things are stuck
or time is being squandered.

Lord of all time,
help me to inhabit time calmly, attending to the pulse
of your grace, the season of your
Spirit and not my own
impatient desire.

Give me confidence and dignity
whenever I am required to wait.
Calm my growing agitation when waiting seems long,
and distract me with glimpses of your purpose
and presence.
Reconcile me to the present moment
and the slow but certain dawning
of your new future.

Monday

Simplicity

Lord, make me simple – for I have become too complicated.
Take from me the vain dreams of sophistication and status,
and give me in return a desire to be shaped by the service
    of others.

Take from me the desire to accumulate or hoard
and give me in return a decluttered life
and simple spirit.

Help me to be content with what is
and with who I am.
Help me to delight in what I see,
what I hear.
Help me to appreciate the people I know well.
Help me to see the stranger's grace.

Give me your gifts of straightforwardness and clarity.
Lead me into integrity.
Pull me from the deceits of shame
and let me become
wholehearted and
transparent.

That when people see through me,
they might glimpse your trace.

Tuesday

Gentleness

God of mist and dew,
of quiet and calm,
of lightness of touch:
help us to be gentle.

Gentle with others.
Gentle with ourselves.
Gentle when anxious.
Gentle when angry.
Gentle in word.
Gentle at work.

Give us, we pray,
the calm that makes for consideration,
the respect for others that makes us courteous.

Give us a good pace of living.
Hold us back when we begin to rush.
Steady us when we panic.

Take from us the coarsening word, the cynical look.
Take from our countenance any expression that could
unsettle one of your vulnerable ones.

God of the Golden Rule,
let us be to others as we need them to be to us.
And let others be to us as we
seek to be to them.

When we fail, forgive us.
When they fail, heal us.

When we hurt each other, reconcile us.

And all by your most gentle grace.

Wednesday

Irony

Lord, we know that it is impossible
that we will ever see ourselves as others see us.
But help us to distance ourselves a little
from our own egos.

Send us the critics and clowns
who will hold a mirror
when we are least presentable.

Send us counsellors and companions
who will care for us,
and goad us into self-awareness.

Send us the friends
who will admire and love us enough to say a word
which allows us to glimpse the self we never want to see.

And give us space, Lord:
space in our minds and in our hearts;
space in which to roam around ourselves;
space enough to let a wry smile of knowing
broaden into a grin;
space enough to let the tear of pity become a lament;
space enough to let in the one or two
others who challenge our complacency.

Give me irony, Lord,
not as a way of disturbing others
or diminishing seriousness.
Give me rather the irony that unsettles my egotism and pride,
that troubles my certainty and
that allows me to laugh and cry
in the company of familiar friends and frightening strangers.
Give me enough irony that allies and enemies may,
in my heart at least,
be reconciled.

Thursday

Courage

Lord of life, I ask for a gift
I never want to need or use:
the gift of courage.

I pray for it for myself, as with uncertainty
I look towards an unknown future,
wondering where and when I will be tested and
fearing that my cowardice will one day be exposed.

I pray it for those who will need it this day.
Those who face threats from others,
the prospect of physical pain, or
exposure to ridicule and embarrassment.

Give me eyes to see beauty, dignity and
grace in the bravery of others.
Help me when I am tempted away from truth and service
by my lack of courage.

Help me to escape the habits and tricks of avoidance.
Rid me, I pray, of all false courage
and dangerous machismo,
of dull stoicism and unfeeling hardness.

Bless me, I pray, with the courage of Gethsemane.

And bind me in the fellowship of those
who take the cup of necessary suffering,
and drink from it.

Friday

Kindness

Although I am grateful,
I rarely appreciate the kindness of others
as deeply or as warmly as I should.

Help me to be attentive to the kindness which comes to me,
for the small courtesies and considerations,
for the delicate movements of graceful politeness.

Help me, I pray, to remain kind in my words and in my attitudes,
in my habits and in my spontaneous actions.

Give me a kindly spirit,
kind words
and a kind heart.
Save me from the cynical and cruel tendencies which lie within.

Save me too from being anodyne or dull.
Save me most of all from the curse of patronizing niceness.
May I be neither a giver nor a receiver
of anything bland or diminishing.
Make me robust and kind,
honest and kind,
compassionate and kind.

Make me a good companion to others, many others,
whether our time together is marked
by decades or seconds.

Give me the gift of kindness.

Saturday

Generosity

God of grace, giver of all good things,
fount of creation and source of love,
we pray that we might become people of generosity.

Teach us how to give,
and teach us the many ways in which giving can be possible
    for us.

Our hearts are often anxious, fearing that we have too little
    to give.
Help us to see that your provision is more than adequate,
and that your abundance is reached only as we share in
    your generosity.

Give us, we pray, the inclination and the resolve to be generous
with our provisions.
Help us to share our food with the hungry.
Help us to be generous with our time –
patient with those who make us wait,
attentive to those who need us to listen,
calm and positive with those who need our
instruction, direction or explanation.

Enable us to be generous with our money,
finding creative and transformative ways to give.
Make us open-handed and yet responsible
givers of financial support.

Give us generosity of spirit:
positive, accommodating,
gracious in attitude,
slow to judge,
quick to honour, praise and bless,
sincere in word and gesture.

By your grace help us to give of ourselves.
It seems to us a mean offering,
but it is the best we have.

Help us to let go of our desire to control.
Let us abandon ourselves to your will
with a smile of uncertainty on our lips
but with the joy of faith in our hearts.

Week 7

DEEPS

————◦•◦————

Where spirituality and prayer are not deep, we might wonder whether they are spirituality and prayer at all. 'Out of the depths', said the Psalmist, 'I cry to you, O LORD. Lord, hear my voice!' (Psalm 130).

Our prayer does not always begin deep. Indeed a very good place to begin might well be the shallow end. Honest prayer is better than dishonest. If your honest concerns are at the shallow end of the spiritual pond, or even more at home in the paddling pool . . . that's where you begin. Depth matters, and we will come, sooner or later, to the infinitely deep ocean of God's love. Yet honesty matters more. That is why *responses* precede *virtues* and *deeps* in this collection. Prayer as the response to circumstance, our own and that of others, is true prayer, and much less liable to distraction. 'People on sinking ships,' wrote Herbert McCabe, 'do not complain of distractions during their prayer.'*

Twentieth-century theology, troubled as it inevitably was by wars and philosophy, science and technology, sought out

————

* H. McCabe, *God, Christ and Us* (London: Continuum, 2003), p. 8.

metaphors of depth to describe God. Phrases like 'Ultimate Reality' and 'Ground of Being' were coined in the study and migrated to the pulpit and even the hymnal; but on their own are too dry and abstract to be appropriated in prayer. They are hardly the language of the beating heart or fretful spirit. Jesus does not call out to Ultimate Reality from the cross, nor does he argue with the Ground of Being in Gethsemane.

Holy Week is an encounter with depth. The invitation is there in the Lamentations of Jeremiah: 'see if there is any sorrow like my sorrow' (Lamentations 1.12). The invitation is not only to see and hear again, but to enter more deeply into that which is infinitely deep. This is the task of prayer, and it is by prayer that we can be honest about our *too-difficult tray*, articulate the pain of our pain, wrestle with the cross, and come to a place of timeless contemplation while we await that which we cannot yet begin to imagine. If this involves us going underground to mine the spirit or enter into the darkest cave of the soul, we can only say, 'So be it.'

Palm Sunday

Hosanna

It's not like me to shout –
    honestly.
But then:
it's not like a Messiah to come –
    humbly.

Humble Messiah,
hear our hosannas today.
Hear us and help us.
Hear us and heal us.
Accept all that we throw at you:
our garments,
these branches,
the shouts
that come from our hearts, our
sharply broken hearts.

Heroic Son of David:
heal us, and
give us the hope we cannot grasp.

Holy Son of David:
heal us, and
open the gate of heaven.

Humble Son of David:
heal us, and
let us follow.

Monday

Pain

Today the subject of my prayer
is easy to find. I don't need to look
or search; it finds me.

More than that, it seeks me and traps
me; holds me where I don't like
to be held. It's not the only thing
on my mind,
but it's so tenacious,
far more tenacious than me,
I fear.

Yes, I fear.

The pain I experience
awakens before me, before the dawn,
and summons my
slumbering mind to a grudging alertness.

This is what I hate about pain:
not the pain itself – not the hurt in it,
though that's bad enough.
It's the attention it demands.
The fact that I can't forget it, can't
clear it from my mind, can't get beyond it,
behind it, around it. I am not even sure that
I will get through it.

The pain, it seems, is in
my mind as much as in
my body: sometimes it's
chronic, sometimes intermittent,
always gnawing. It's not a headache,
it's my mind, my whole mind.

Oh, how I wish it were not so!
Oh, how I hate the feel of pain!
Even now I despise myself for feeling it!
How I long to overcome it!

Yet the truth is that the
pain overcomes
me. It invades, vanquishes and
diminishes me.

And this is the worst. It's the pain
that melts my prayer, dissipates
my spirit, undermines whatever
was solid in my soul. It's the
pain that returns me not to
flights of faith but to the
rude reality of the physical:
the brute bluntness of the
body.

Save me from the talons which
claw into my mind. Save me from the
searing heat of crumbling bones
and flayed flesh.

Save me from the brilliant
electric brightness, and the deep
delayed explosion:

the internal thunderstorm which
known to me alone
is all I know,
and which I am all
the more alone for knowing.

Save me: and be with all in pain
this day and this night.

Tuesday

Untie My Depths

My mind is still,
my body is at rest;
you are my desire.
But I am alone;

alone with a knot –
a knot in my depths.
A tight, congested inner tangle.
I would love to tease it out.

I pull a strand,
the whole knot tightens.
I leave it alone.
It does not go away.

I raise my feelings to my throat,
the energy is caught below.
I raise my thoughts high in my head,
they are anchored to the knot.

What is this multi-threaded mass?
Who or what makes its rest here?
It drags me down, seals me within,
constricts my soul.

Disentangle me, Lord.
Unpick my inner knot.
Unravel my complexity.
Unweave my deepest confusion.
Untwist the channels of spirit within.

Pull apart the strands.
Prune the nuisance strings.
See my spiritual sclerosis and
soften, soften,
soften.

Stretch me from without.
Bless me from above.
Breathe your Spirit through me
and, by your mercy,
untie my depths.

Wednesday

Monochrome

Maybe it's because I don't remember
in colour, that black
and white photographs seem to me
more truthful.

Trees and fields are more their
textured selves.
Skies, often a vague background
grey, are less imposing.
The cut of the suit, lounge or
bathing, more vividly indicates not year but
era.

Even on a small photo, and
some are very small, faces
feel more vivid, expressions
more personal and acute. Less prepared.
A slight difference in eyebrow
deportment – an entirely different
atmosphere, mood, memory.

Colour tells too
much, too easily misleads. It
closes down too soon.
Monochrome says 'colour me in'.
It seeks not my admiration
but my participation.

Let me be, then, more
black and white in who I am,
what I say, what I do.
Not clotting into any dogmatic either/or
but, in the unfinishedness
of what I put in front of others,
let me contribute boldly,
within a frame, and
within the limits of monochrome
possibility.
Let me risk looking dull in the
cause of exploration and adventure.
Let me live with constraint
that others may transcend.
Let me be grey
that others may
colour and be
coloured.

Maundy Thursday

Too Difficult

I have a special place, so secret I
myself can never remember where to find it,
where I put these things.
An anti-treasure chest into which I
throw, hurl or, more often, surreptitiously
slip all the tasks I dread,
all the words I know I need to say but
cannot.
The problems in that box are
intractable.
The people trapped therein have mouths
which gape, like chicks in a nest.
They want the food I don't have,
I cannot find.
It's as busy as an ants' hill in there.
A beehive filled with sour honey; the
wax of the comb is rancid through neglect.
It's a compost heap, a pile of damp
grass – in danger of self-combusting as
the temperature rises.
I cannot put my hand in there. It's a home for a
hornet; the viper hides there,
warming for a venture.

Take me to this place, slowly and boldly.
Take me to this place.
There is no time to prepare. All preparation
is distraction. Distraction is
what keeps this place so
fetid and toxic.

Take me there and let me put my
hand into that mess.
Let me risk the scratches, bites, abrasions,
burns.
Let me find from that corner of chaos one thing,
and perhaps a second,
to which I can give some attention,
some time, some effort.
Let me extract from that pit
just one torment
that by grace it might be tamed.
Let me look there for some
filament on which to pull.
Let me find the way
to unloosen the window and let
in light and air.

Yes, it is too much to ask.
Yes, it is too difficult. That's the point.
Give me the grace to do the difficult thing
today.

Good Friday

Mysterious Cross

Unfamiliar cross,
I know your shape, your form.
Your meaning has been my study year
on year.
Yet I know you not.

Symbol of reconciliation,
of love, of grace.
Why do you push me back?
Why alienate me so?

Your face – always new.
Your arms – always open.
Your foot – always planted.
Your mouth – always shut.

Others gaze on you and pass by satisfied.
They understand you fully,
whether bare wood or body hung,
whether sculpted, or in oils;
they read your surface and move on.

Mysterious cross,
you hold my stare, reflect it back.
Your unfathomable eyes, like the blackest
of holes,
draw me in, draw me deep.

Speak, silent cross!
Proclaim, strangest one!
Whisper some comfort.
Breathe out, at last, with consolation.

You have me nailed.
Not with iron but by a
dart of love.
You have me transfixed.

Let me be
transformed.

Holy Saturday

Contemplation

I have kept myself still
before you.
The flood of ideas is stemmed.
The carnival of images has passed.
The fragments of music quietened.

Words have come,
chosen and repeated;
unbidden, uttered and
sent on their way.

Now the quiet is ascendant.
I have no question,
no request,
no petition,
no penitence,
no praise.

Out of the deep a phrase
emerges; like a bubble
it floats to the surface and bursts.
Others will come,
but they are few.
I let them pass,
let them go.

The tick of the clock,
such a steadying rhythm,
does not need my attention
after all. It does
not get it.

I move my fingers and toes to
ensure I am not asleep.
That my will can command.
It can.
It chooses not to.

I remain in your peace.
I absorb your peace.
I will rise, in due course,
to live your peace.

For now, for this
timeless, timed now,
silence is poised peace.
I offer it as my prayer.

Week 8

HORIZONS

———•◆•———

Easter changes the map of human understanding.

Yes, it is an intellectual trauma as great as that. It rips up reality and replaces it with *Reality*. It is not so much out with the old and in with the new as out with the understood and in with the mysterious; out with the limited and in with the unlimited; out with the possible and in with the impossible. To call Easter a revolution is to understate it. Resurrection is the only word – and it is a word that implies death.

What does this mean for our prayer?

We cannot say precisely, of course, because we cannot know precisely; we cannot tie it down.

And there, perhaps, is the clue.

Easter invites us to loosen our prayer yet more, to ease our intended grip. Easter invites us to shake off the shackles, to untie the grave clothes, to roll the stone from the door of our heart and let the Spirit spring forth. More than this – to let the resurrected body spring forth.

For us mortals, however, those on this side of the grave – I mean those of us who are still somewhere in the passage between birth and death – Easter prayer will always have one foot in ordinary, contingent, unredeemed life. Traumatically transformative as it is, Easter is for us part of the everyday. Easter now is not only 'in ordinarie', as George Herbert put it.* It *is* 'ordinary'. The Eucharist is our *pain quotidien* and our *vin de pays*.

Yet the paradox is stark. The glimpse of glory that we see, the trace of triumph, the hint of victory, is so new to us that we just can't fathom it.

And so we come to prayers that press at our limits and our horizons. Prayers that creep slowly out from the ragged sheets of the freshly torn up map of all that we thought we knew. Prayers that we might relocate relationships with others and ourselves, prayers that accept and transcend our own limit of bodily death, and prayers that reach out to God's infinity as the ultimate Thou and the cause, reason and justification of our use of the most pregnant and powerful of all prayers, the simple *Amen*.

---

* In his poem 'Prayer'; H. Wilcox (ed.), *The English Poems of George Herbert* (Cambridge: Cambridge University Press, 2007), p. 178.

Easter Sunday

———◆◆◆———

Embracing the Mystery

Although I long to understand . . .
Although I long to know . . .
Although I fancy wisdom . . .
Although I crave the light . . .
I know how little I know.
I know how often I am confused,
confounded,
muddled.

Help me to be clear about this at least:
that I know little;
that I miss more than I see;
that I am surprised more often,
far more often, than
I ever admit.

I love days of blue skies and clear horizons.
I love the clear map, the vivid description.
I love the clear instruction,
the quick result,
the method that works, the prediction that comes true.

I love that resonance when a story or a poem
unfolds with insights already
familiar.
I love the thrill of recognition:
I know that,

I know this,
I know you,
I know them.
I love to know why,
how,
where
and when.

Alas, it is so rarely like this,
'tis *never* thus.

The mountain range of knowledge:
hidden in mist from me.
I see a foothill, and know that every summit is false.
I walk over rock. I can't even begin to
understand its story.
I see the planets – how many can I name?
Can I say how the winds reshape the clouds?

The night-time journey. I
imagine a clear path, an open road,
floodlights, headlights, clear signs.
I find myself in a Devon lane:
high hedges, sharp bends, cloudy sky,
no moon, no stars.
The headlights have broken, sidelights
only glow in the dark.

Yet I do see a little.
But no, not enough.
Not nearly enough.
The light: a single, flickering, vulnerable
flame, the sun diffused through mist, a dim torch
making its own horizon.

I need to see more, know more,
understand better.

Unless, unless, unless . . .
I accept it.
Accept the truth of my lack of vision,
my lack of wisdom and understanding, and
begin to learn how to walk: to develop
the confidence, courage and patience
simply to put one foot in front of the other.

And so I pray:
not for wisdom,
not to see more,
not to understand better,
not to find life predictable,
not to be the one who knows . . .
but for the grace
to see enough through my own beclouded eyes,
to accept the morning mist in my mind
and to walk into
mystery.

Monday

O Thou!

O beginning!
O beauty!
O brilliance!

O wonder!
O presence!
O silence!

O mercy!
O wholeness!
O healing!

O energy!
O darkness!
O glory!

O friend!
O end!
O Thou!

Tuesday

Reconciliation

We are standing apart.
Too far apart to touch – thank goodness.
We face each other but don't see
the face.
We look over. We look through.
We look at. We look beyond. We look askance.
What!

There is a gulf here.
A chasm.
A fjord.
A grand canyon.
A sea.
Tectonic plates below us,
moved by forces unknown and unstoppable,
pull us apart
inexorably.
Perhaps it is for the best.
If we are distant enough
avoidance will take no effort,
bring us the peace of forgetting.

Let this not be!
I cannot 'Amen' my own prayer.
I see no future if I turn my back.
The future is in the face I

strive not to see in my shadowy moments,
dreams,
in the cracked mirror of my erstwhile
hopes.

I have made an other of you.
And you have made an other of me.

Let us see that, at least.
And let us learn to look again.
To strain our eyes to the horizon;
to see the outline of the form;
to see the shape of the face;
to see the colour of the eyes;
to read the anguish of the soul;
to read the hope, the aspiration, the desire,
that makes no sense to us,
no sense at all.

Send us forward to that place where
we can forget the forlorn peace of
forgetting,
where we can remember well, and look
kindly.

Where we can know
the peace of truth and the judgement of
mercy.
Not through understanding all,
but by accepting the wound of mental
other-ing.

Wednesday

Joy

I have a sinking feeling
that when I look back over my
life, from the distance of great years,
or the moment when I know the crash will be
fatal, or the seconds when the heart beats
its own destruction, or stroke
blanks the mind, or while watching the dread
film of life as salt water
fills my lungs . . . that, on reflection,
my life had a deficit of
joy.

The feeling comes not on the bad days, not
on the days of hard work, straining effort,
not on the days where compassion is stretched, nor even
on the many days of ordinary failure.

It comes on the days of sunlight,
on the days of getting things right,
on the days of deepest delight,
on the days of clearest sight.

Where does it come from, this melancholic
demon of the sublime, this dangerous undercurrent of
exaltation, this gravitational pull on the
spirit, this unbearable heaviness of
soul?

I see dogs running in the field: why can't I run with them,
alive in the moment?
I hear the sound of children at play,
and know that the abandon of playtime is
in my past. The scent of sage comes powerfully
as I crush the leaf, capturing me for a second,
but releasing an inchoate,
unfocused longing. Warmed by the sun my muscles
relax, and then immediately
tense, just
in case.

Elusive, ungraspable joy, let me
glimpse you once more, unreflectingly,
thoughtlessly, timelessly; catch
me unawares and keep my busy-mind
at bay.

Unpredictable, undemanding joy, let me
dissolve into your abundant
sufficiency, your limitless
expansiveness, your eternal,
redemptive fullness.

Limitless joy, release me from self-reflection;
release me into easy
joy; release me into Easter joy, the joy of no
tomorrow,
where tomorrow is
today.

Thursday

Breeze

When there is no breeze,
leaves rest as if they'd
never move.
Smoke rises thin and
vertical, a pencil plume in the sky.

When there is no breeze,
mist smothers the valley,
clouds hang heavy,
humidity swells.

When there is no breeze,
birdsong travels,
footfall thuds,
a scratching squirrel is
an excitement.

When the breeze comes,
faces turn up,
eyebrows quicken,
heartbeat moves from
bass to snare.

When the breeze comes,
mist disperses,
clouds move,
humidity departs.

When the breeze comes,
water ripples,
hair ruffles,
cheeks tingle.

When the breeze comes;
we rise to life.

Friday

Dying

I am poured out like water, gently
flowing over the cusp
of something.
Sometimes a surge,
sometimes a drip, drip, hesitant drip
of life force.
Not slipping away but flowing
inarticulately
on.
Not rising up, but taking the humble,
river-like route,
streaming away,
downhill.

There is no head of steam,
no pressure from within,
no tension, energy or effort.
There is no need to push.
No need to reach
upwards.

I give myself downwards, as stream gives
to river, as river to sea.

Let me not pollute thy vastness
with my solid, insoluble stuff. No, let me
disperse in thy
forgiving wholeness.
Let me be free
in thy great
sea.

Saturday

Amen

Amen:
I have never started a prayer with that word before.
Yet it is right.

Amen:
This one-word sentence says enough.

Amen:
Acceptance. Gratitude. Joy, perhaps.

Amen:
Pause for breath. Look up. Take another step.

Amen:
Desire expressed. Longing left. Hands open.

Amen:
Request for answer. End of me. Over to you.

Thanks

———•◆•———

A small company of people have helped and encouraged with this project – some before there was a project. Karenza Passmore, for instance, gave me a little notebook *for creativity* which kicked this all off. Others responded with warm and difference-making encouragement when they read a small sample of what I had written and asked for more: Bridget Hewitt, Anne Meredith, Caroline Dick, Marian Partington, Judy Hirst, Judy Turner, Anne Lindsley, Jane Nethsingha and Sheryl Shenk. I am extremely grateful to you all.

It was on the Isle of Man that I first dared to share a few of these with people live – and in fact wrote both 'Speaking Day' and 'Listening Day' while there to spend some time with the Island Spirituality Group at the invitation of Canon Peter Robinson. It was an important weekend for me – thank you.

Dame Laurentia Johns of Stanbrook Abbey has been a prayerful companion on the journey of making this collection, and her spiritual generosity has added immeasurably both to my own learning and to the collection itself.

Philip Law, my editor at SPCK, might well have been surprised to have received a few of these prayers by return email when he suggested that we might meet to talk about an altogether different project, but not as surprised as I was with his enthusiasm to use the material in this form. If there is any credit for this book it belongs in good part to Philip.

I am increasingly aware that it is not only the people who contribute directly to a writing project who deserve to be thanked. My diocesan colleagues have taught me so much and my PA,

Mrs Joyce Parker, constantly provides the sanity and sense that help keep me grounded. My Cathedral colleagues are also on my mind as I write this. We are serious about corporate prayer at Durham Cathedral, and over recent years I have been formed by the rhythm of said and sung services and the prayerful creativity of others. I offer my heartfelt thanks for far more than can be expressed here.

This writing really got going when I was away from home on holiday near Assisi with Maggie, who deserves the greatest thanks for sharing the journey and putting up with the wondering, pondering and scribbling which rather over-punctuated a lovely couple of weeks there – and many other days as well.